Fun Facts
for Kids

500 FUNNY AND MIND-BLOWING FACTS ABOUT DINOSAURS, SPACE, SPORTS, AND EVERYTHING ELSE IN BETWEEN

RILEY WOLFE

Published by Astro Story Scope

FREE BONUS

SCAN THIS TO GET OUR NEXT

BOOK FOR FREE!

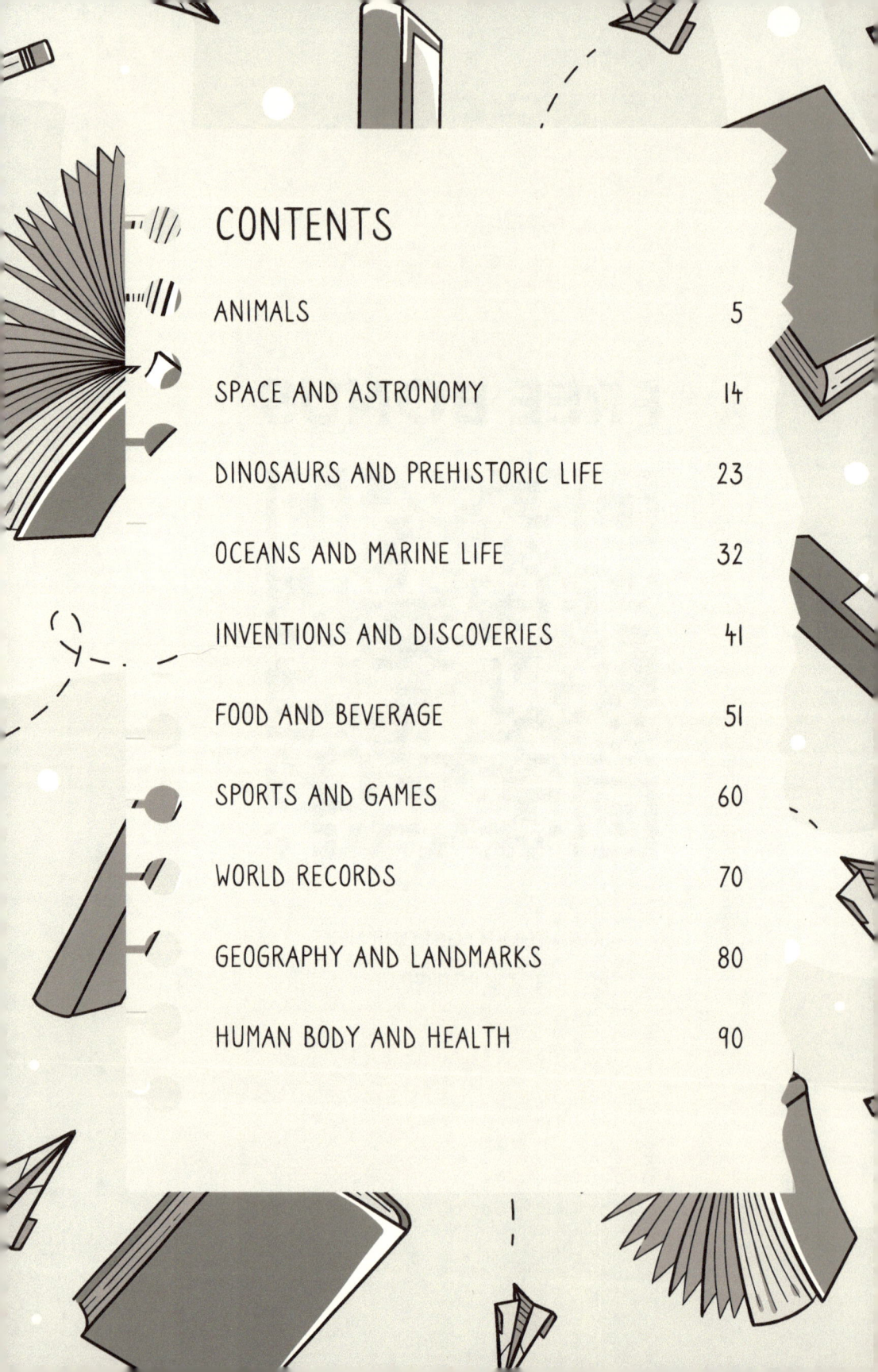

CONTENTS

ANIMALS

FUN FACTS FOR KIDS

1   Did you know that a grizzly bear's bite is so strong, it could crush a bowling ball? Talk about a bear hug!

2   The tongue of a blue whale is so big that 50 people could stand on it. Imagine the selfies!

3   A shrimp's heart is in its head. No wonder they're called "shrimp-brained"!

4   Did you know that cows have best friends? They like to hang out with their buddies and moo-ve together!

5   Penguins can't fly, but they sure can swim! They're like the torpedoes of the animal world.

6   The sailfish is the fastest swimmer in the ocean, reaching speeds of up to 68 mph! That's faster than most cars on the highway.

7   You might think chameleons change color to match their surroundings, but they actually change color based on their mood. Talk about wearing your emotions on your sleeve!

8 The world's smallest mammal is the bumblebee bat. It's so tiny it could fit on the tip of your finger!

9 Did you know that giraffes have the same number of neck bones as humans? They just have really, really long ones!

10 Some frogs can freeze during the winter and thaw out in the spring, good as new! Talk about a long nap!

11 A snail can sleep for up to three years. Now that's a lazy Sunday!

12 Did you know that crocodiles can live up to 100 years? They've got serious staying power!

13 A group of jellyfish is called a smack. It's like they're giving each other a high five!

14 A group of porcupines is called a prickle. Watch out, they're a bit "pointy"!

15 Seahorses are the only animals where the male gives birth! Dad seahorses carry the eggs in a special pouch.

16 Koalas sleep up to 22 hours a day. They're the ultimate nap champions!

17 The cheetah can accelerate faster than most sports cars, reaching speeds of 60 mph in just 3 seconds!

18 The bat is the only mammal that can truly fly. They're like the superheroes of the animal kingdom!

19 Elephants can recognize themselves in a mirror. They must love taking selfies!

20 An octopus has three hearts and blue blood. Talk about being unique!

21 A kangaroo can't walk backward. They're always moving forward, just like you!

22 A star-nosed mole can eat worms faster than the human eye can follow. It's like a magic trick!

23 Giraffes only need 5 to 30 minutes of sleep per day. Imagine all the extra time they have for midnight snacks!

24 Owls can turn their heads almost all the way around, up to 270 degrees. They've got eyes in the back of their heads!

25 A rhinoceros beetle can lift up to 850 times its own weight. That's like a human lifting two elephants!

26 The dung beetle can navigate by the stars. They're like tiny, poop-loving astronomers!

27 Flamingos get their pink color from the food they eat, like shrimp and algae. It's like they're wearing their dinner!

28 Sloths only poop once a week, and it's a big event! They do a little "poo dance" before getting down to business.

29 The slow loris has a venomous bite. It's like a cute, cuddly, and dangerous teddy bear!

30 The horned lizard can shoot blood out of its eyes to scare off predators. Talk about a creepy superpower!

31 The mimic octopus can change its shape and color to look like other animals. It's like the master of disguise!

32 The pangolin is the only mammal covered in scales. They're like walking pinecones!

33 The blobfish looks like a sad, squishy blob when out of water, but in its deep-sea home, it looks like a regular fish. It's all about perspective!

34 The basilisk lizard can run on water, earning it the nickname "Jesus lizard." It's a miracle worker!

35 A cat's purr can help heal bones and tissues. They're like furry little doctors!

36 Dogs have a sense of smell that's 10,000 to 100,000 times stronger than humans. They could sniff out your hidden candy stash from miles away!

37 Some ants can explode to protect their colony. They're like living firecrackers!

38 The male lyrebird can mimic almost any sound, including chainsaws and camera shutters. It's like a living, breathing soundboard!

39 The narwhal's tusk is actually a long, spiral tooth that can grow up to 10 feet long. They're like the unicorns of the sea!

40 The tapeworm can grow up to 30 feet long inside a host's body. Yikes! That's longer than a school bus!

41 A kangaroo can't jump if you lift its tail off the ground. It's like their superpower is being switched off with the flick of a tail!

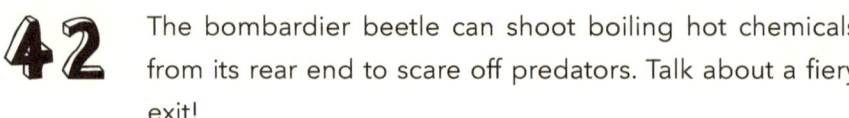

42 The bombardier beetle can shoot boiling hot chemicals from its rear end to scare off predators. Talk about a fiery exit!

43 A male peacock's feathers are so bright and colorful to attract a mate. It's like wearing your fanciest outfit to impress your crush!

44 The proboscis monkey has a huge, droopy nose that can grow up to 7 inches long. They're the Pinocchios of the animal world!

45 Ostriches have the largest eyes of any land animal. With eyes that big, they must never miss a thing at their bird-watching parties!

46 A single ant can carry up to 50 times its own body weight. It's like they have their very own ant-sized weightlifting championships!

47 The tongue of a woodpecker wraps around its brain to protect it from damage while pecking. Talk about a built-in helmet!

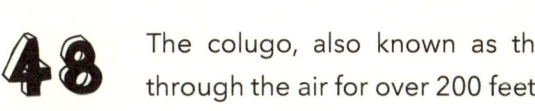

48 The colugo, also known as the flying lemur, can glide through the air for over 200 feet. It's like a living kite!

49 The mantis shrimp can see colors that humans can't even imagine. They must think our world is pretty boring!

50 Squirrels can't burp or vomit. They must be the most polite dinner guests in the animal kingdom!

SPACE AND ASTRONOMY

1 Space is completely silent because there's no air to carry sound waves. If an alien sneezed, you wouldn't hear a thing!

2 There's a volcano on Mars called Olympus Mons, which is so tall, it's nearly 3 times the height of Earth's Mount Everest. Don't pull a muscle looking up!

3 The sun is so big that you could fit about 1.3 million Earths inside it. That's a lot of beach vacations!

4 A neutron star is so dense that just a teaspoon of its material would weigh about as much as a mountain! Imagine that on a weight scale!

5 Did you know that the moon is slowly moving away from Earth at about the same speed that your fingernails grow? A turtle moves faster!

6 Saturn is so light that if you could find a big enough bathtub, it would float in the water! Don't forget the rubber duckies!

7 In space, astronauts grow taller because there's no gravity to compress their spines. They become real-life stretchy toys!

8 The Great Red Spot on Jupiter is a giant storm that's been raging for over 300 years. Talk about a never-ending bad hair day!

9 Earth's atmosphere makes our sunsets look red and orange because it scatters light. It's like nature's own Instagram filter!

10 The footprints left by astronauts on the moon will be there for millions of years because there's no wind or water to wash them away. No tornadoes to worry about there!

11 A year on Pluto lasts 248 Earth years, which means if you lived there, you'd have a birthday party every 248 years. Better make it a big one!

12 If two pieces of the same type of metal touch in space, they will stick together permanently. It's like cosmic superglue!

13 A day on Mercury lasts 1,408 Earth hours. Talk about a never-ending workday!

14 There's a planet called HD 189733b where it rains glass sideways. Bring your toughest umbrella!

15 Space has a smell! Astronauts describe it as a mix of hot metal, welding fumes, and barbecue. Barbecue ribs, anyone?

16 The Milky Way has over 200 billion stars, and there are trillions of galaxies in the observable universe. Talk about a big neighborhood!

17 Uranus spins on its side, like a rolling ball rather than a spinning top. It must have had one crazy cosmic collision!

18 The temperature on the moon can go from boiling hot to freezing cold in just a couple of hours. That's some serious mood swings!

19 Some scientists think there might be a giant, hidden planet in our solar system called Planet Nine. Maybe it's just shy!

20 The International Space Station is the largest man-made object in space and can sometimes be seen from Earth with the naked eye.

21 A full NASA space suit costs around 12 million dollars. That's one expensive outfit!

22 Halley's Comet only comes around once every 75 years. How old will you be 75 years from now?

23 The speed of light is approximately 186,282 miles per second. That's faster than Superman!

24 There are more stars in the universe than there are grains of sand on all the beaches on Earth. That's a whole lot of sunbathing spots!

25 There's a planet made of diamonds called 55 Cancri e, which is twice the size of Earth. Talk about a girl's best friend!

26 Astronauts in space can't cry properly because there's no gravity to help the tears flow. They just end up with watery eyeballs!

27 Our galaxy, the Milky Way, is on a collision course with our neighboring galaxy, Andromeda. Don't worry, it won't happen for another 4.5 billion years!

28 If you unraveled all of your DNA, it would stretch from the Earth to the sun and back about 600 times. You're literally full of cosmic potential!

29 In 2006, the International Astronomical Union decided that Pluto wasn't a planet anymore, but a dwarf planet. Poor Pluto!

30 Neptune has the strongest winds in our solar system, reaching speeds of up to 1,200 miles per hour. Hold on to your hats!

31 Astronauts have to exercise for at least two hours a day in space to prevent muscle and bone loss due to the lack of gravity. Imagine the view from that gym!

32 A day on Mars is 39 minutes and 35 seconds longer than a day on Earth. Think of all the extra things you could do with that time!

33 If you could drive to the moon at a speed of 60 miles per hour, it would take you about six months to get there. Better pack a lunch!

34 Did you know that astronauts eat food that comes in tubes, like toothpaste? That's one small bite for man, one giant squeeze for mankind!

35 Astronomers have discovered a planet that orbits two stars, just like Tatooine in Star Wars. May the force be with you!

36 Mars has the largest dust storms in our solar system. They can last for months and cover the entire planet!

37 Jupiter's moon Europa might have more water than Earth! Who's up for an intergalactic swim?

38 Jupiter's moon Europa might have more water than Earth! Who's up for an intergalactic swim?

39 The sun is so far away that it takes eight minutes and 20 seconds for its light to reach us on Earth. Talk about a long-distance relationship!

40 The first animals to go into space were fruit flies, sent up in 1947. They were followed by monkeys, dogs, and eventually humans. Talk about a wild space adventure!

41 In 1969, a flag was planted on the moon during the Apollo 11 mission. Due to the lack of atmosphere, it still stands there today, but the colors have faded to white. It's like a ghostly flag waving in space!

42 Earth's atmosphere protects us from most of the meteors that come our way, burning them up before they can hit the ground. It's like our planet's invisible shield!

43 Astronauts on the International Space Station see 16 sunrises and sunsets every day. Talk about a room with a view!

44 Black holes have such strong gravity that not even light can escape them. It's like a cosmic vacuum cleaner, except what goes in, never comes out!

45 Mars has the longest canyon in the solar system, Valles Marineris. It's so big you could fit the entire Grand Canyon inside it 20 times!

46 The first pizza ever delivered to space was in 2001. Talk about a special delivery!

 In 2013, astronaut Chris Hadfield recorded the first music video in space. Talk about reaching for the stars!

 Venus is the hottest planet in our solar system, even though Mercury is closer to the sun. Looks like Venus can't keep its cool!

 The Pistol Star is one of the most luminous stars in the Milky Way. It's so bright that if it were as close to Earth as the sun, we'd need sunglasses 24/7!

 The dwarf planet Haumea, located beyond Neptune, is shaped like a football and completes a rotation every 3.9 hours. Touchdown in the cosmos!

DINOSAURS AND PREHISTORIC LIFE

1 The word "dinosaur" means "terrible lizard" in Greek, but don't worry - they're not around anymore to be terrible!

2 The Stegosaurus had a brain the size of a walnut, even though its body was the size of a van. Talk about a small thinker!

3 The Tyrannosaurus rex had teeth as long as bananas. Imagine trying to brush those chompers!

4 The first flowers appeared on Earth around 130 million years ago during the Cretaceous period. It's like nature's first bouquet!

5 Some dinosaurs, like the Velociraptor, had feathers. They were like giant, scaly birds!

6 The smallest dinosaur ever discovered was only the size of a chicken. Watch out for your toes!

7 The Argentinosaurus was so big that its footsteps could create mini-earthquakes. It's like a living, breathing wrecking ball!

8 The Ankylosaurus had a club-like tail that it used to defend itself. Talk about a prehistoric weapon!

9 The Spinosaurus was even bigger than the T. rex and could swim! It's like the ultimate pool party crasher.

10 The Triceratops had three horns on its face, which it used for defense and maybe even attracting mates. What a fancy facial accessory!

11 The Pterosaurs were flying reptiles, not actually dinosaurs, but they lived at the same time. They were like the prehistoric air force!

12 The Maiasaura, a plant-eating dinosaur, was a very caring parent. They even built nests for their eggs, just like modern-day birds.

13 Some dinosaurs had sharp, curved claws to help them climb trees. Talk about prehistoric tree huggers!

14 The Brachiosaurus had nostrils on top of its head. Imagine having to blow your nose up there!

15 During the Devonian period, Earth was home to the first trees, called Archaeopteris. They were the ancient pioneers of modern forests!

16 The biggest dinosaur eggs ever found were as big as basketballs. That's one giant omelet!

17 The Microraptor had four wings, making it a unique flier in the dinosaur world. It's like a prehistoric biplane!

18 The Oviraptor got its name because it was once thought to steal eggs, but it turns out it was just a caring parent guarding its nest. Oops!

19 The Woolly Mammoth lived during the Ice Age and had long, curved tusks perfect for shoveling snow. It's like a prehistoric snowplow!

20 The giant, prehistoric shark called Megalodon had teeth the size of a human hand. No swimming with this shark!

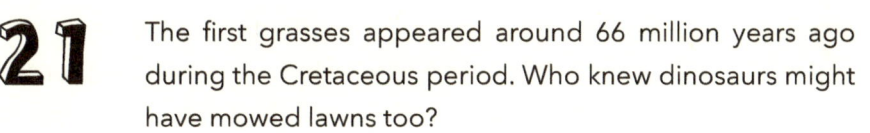

21 The first grasses appeared around 66 million years ago during the Cretaceous period. Who knew dinosaurs might have mowed lawns too?

22 Some dinosaurs, like the Parasaurolophus, had hollow crests on their heads that they may have used to make sounds. It's like a prehistoric trumpet!

23 The Iguanodon was one of the first dinosaurs ever discovered, and it had a thumb spike that it probably used for self-defense. Thumbs up for safety!

24 The Compsognathus was a tiny, fast-running dinosaur that might have hunted insects. Imagine having one of those as a bug zapper!

25 The Pachycephalosaurus had a thick, bony dome on its head, which it may have used for head-butting contests. Talk about a prehistoric headache!

26 The Archaeopteryx is considered the "missing link" between dinosaurs and birds, with features of both. It's like the ultimate prehistoric hybrid!

27 During the Carboniferous period, Earth's atmosphere had a higher oxygen concentration, which may have contributed to the enormous size of insects and other arthropods. Breathe it in!

28 The Troodon was one of the smartest dinosaurs, with a brain-to-body ratio similar to modern birds. Who says dinosaurs were all brawn and no brains?

29 The Titanoboa was a massive snake that could grow up to 40 feet long and weigh over a ton. Talk about a prehistoric slither!

30 The Coelacanth, a prehistoric fish thought to be extinct, was rediscovered in 1938. It's like a living fossil that came back from the past!

31 The giant ground sloth, called Megatherium, lived during the Ice Age and was as big as an elephant. Imagine a slow-moving, cuddly giant!

32 The Ankylosaurus was like a prehistoric tank, with a heavily armored body and a club-like tail for defense. No one would mess with this dino!

33 The Spinosaurus was even bigger than the T. rex and had a large sail on its back. It was like a prehistoric sailboat with teeth!

34 The Velociraptor was about the size of a turkey, despite what movies might show. The real Jurassic Park would be more like a petting zoo!

35 The Argentinosaurus was one of the longest dinosaurs, reaching up to 100 feet in length. It's like a prehistoric stretch limo!

36 The Woolly Mammoth roamed the earth during the Ice Age and was covered in thick, shaggy hair. It's like a prehistoric woolly blanket on legs!

37 The Hesperornis was a prehistoric diving bird that swam in the ocean and had sharp teeth. It's like a penguin with a bite!

38 The first trees appeared during the Devonian period, around 385 million years ago. These ancient trees had no leaves, only branches covered in tiny, photosynthesizing structures. Imagine the shade!

39 The Brachiosaurus had a long neck and could reach up to 85 feet tall. It's like the prehistoric version of a giraffe!

40 The Compsognathus was a tiny, fast-running dinosaur that was about the size of a chicken. It's like the prehistoric roadrunner, but with more teeth!

41 The Dimetrodon was a pre-dinosaur reptile with a sail on its back that helped regulate its body temperature. It's like a prehistoric lizard with its own built-in air conditioning!

42 The Dunkleosteus was an armored fish that lived over 350 million years ago. It's like a prehistoric fish with its own suit of armor!

43 The Coelophysis was one of the earliest known dinosaurs and had hollow bones, similar to modern birds. It's like the prehistoric ancestor of the birds in your backyard!

44 The Amargasaurus was a small sauropod dinosaur with a row of tall spines along its neck and back. It's like a prehistoric punk rocker with a spiky mohawk!

 The Megaloceros, also known as the Irish Elk, was a giant deer with enormous antlers. It's like a prehistoric reindeer, but without the red nose!

 The Dire Wolf was a prehistoric carnivore that lived during the last Ice Age. It's like a wolf, but bigger, stronger, and more ferocious!

 Palm trees first appeared around 80 million years ago, during the late Cretaceous period. Their descendants are still around today. Talk about a tropical vacation!

 The Eoraptor was one of the earliest known dinosaurs, living around 230 million years ago. It's like a prehistoric great-great-great-grandpa of all the other dinos!

 During the Carboniferous Period, giant insects like dragonflies with 2.5-foot wingspans and 8-foot long millipedes roamed the Earth. It's like a prehistoric bug's paradise!

 Cave paintings created by prehistoric humans give us a glimpse into their lives and the animals they lived alongside. It's like a prehistoric art gallery!

OCEANS
AND MARINE LIFE

1 Did you know that 70% of Earth's surface is covered by water? That's a lot of room for splashing around!

2 The Great Barrier Reef in Australia is the largest living structure on Earth. It's so big that it can be seen from space!

3 The Pacific Ocean is the largest ocean on Earth. It's so big that you could fit all of the Earth's landmass inside it and still have room to spare!

4 The Mariana Trench is the deepest part of the ocean, reaching a depth of over 36,000 feet. That's deeper than Mount Everest is tall!

5 The ocean is home to the world's smallest fish, the Paedocypris progenetica, which is only 0.3 inches long. It's like a teeny-tiny swimming grain of rice!

6 The world's largest fish is the whale shark, which can grow up to 40 feet long. That's as long as a school bus!

7   There are underwater mountains called seamounts that are taller than any mountain on land. They're like the secret skyscrapers of the sea!

8   Some fish, like the anglerfish, have a built-in fishing rod and lure on their heads to catch prey. Talk about a handy snack!

9   The immortal jellyfish can revert to an earlier stage of its life cycle and start over again. It's like hitting the "reset" button on life!

10   The blobfish, often called the world's ugliest fish, looks like a big, pink blob when it's out of water. But in its natural deep-sea habitat, it looks like a regular fish!

11   The sailfish is the fastest fish in the ocean, reaching speeds of up to 68 miles per hour. It's like the underwater version of a race car!

12   There are underwater rivers and lakes in the ocean, made up of denser, saltier water. It's like a secret world within a world!

13 The box jellyfish is one of the most venomous creatures on Earth. Its sting can be fatal to humans, so watch out for those tentacles!

14 The giant squid has the largest eyes in the animal kingdom, measuring up to 10 inches in diameter. It's like having dinner plates for eyes!

15 The pistol shrimp can snap its claw so fast that it creates a shockwave that stuns its prey. It's like having a built-in water gun!

16 The ocean sunfish, or mola mola, can lay up to 300 million eggs at once. That's one big fishy family!

17 The mantis shrimp has powerful claws that can smash through glass and even crack crab shells. It's like the superhero of the shrimp world!

18 The narwhal is sometimes called the "unicorn of the sea" because of its long, spiral tusk. But unlike unicorns, narwhals are real!

19 The humpback whale has the longest flippers of any whale, reaching up to 16 feet long. It's like having giant water wings!

20 Sea cucumbers can shoot their internal organs out of their bodies to scare off predators. Talk about a gross defense mechanism!

21 The dumbo octopus, named after the Disney character, has big, ear-like fins that it uses to swim. It's like a cute, underwater elephant!

22 The electric eel can produce an electric shock of up to 600 volts. It's like a living, swimming battery!

23 The deep-sea dragonfish has a lure on its chin that lights up and uses it to attract prey in the dark ocean depths. It's like a living, swimming flashlight!

24 The ocean is home to the world's smallest marine mammal, the vaquita porpoise, which is only about 5 feet long. It's like a mini-dolphin!

25 Coral reefs are made up of millions of tiny animals called coral polyps, which build the reef's structure over thousands of years. It's like a giant, underwater city!

26 The male seahorse is the one that gets pregnant and gives birth to the babies, not the female! Talk about a role reversal!

27 The stonefish is the world's most venomous fish, hiding in plain sight on the ocean floor. Watch your step!

28 The Greenland shark is one of the slowest-moving sharks and can live for up to 400 years. It's like the wise old grandpa of the sea!

29 Some sea turtles can hold their breath for up to 5 hours. That's one impressive set of lungs!

30 The blue whale is the largest animal that has ever lived, reaching up to 100 feet long and weighing as much as 200 tons. It's like a living, swimming jumbo jet!

31 The Atlantic puffin can hold over 60 fish in its beak at once. It's like a walking, squawking sushi platter!

32 The Colossal squid has the largest beak of any squid species. It's like having a giant pair of scissors for a mouth!

33 The Portuguese man o' war is not a jellyfish but a colony of individual organisms called zooids. They all work together like one big, stinging team!

34 Some species of shark, like the hammerhead, have a special organ that can detect electrical fields. It's like having a built-in radar detector!

35 The Pacific barreleye fish has a transparent head that allows it to see through its skull. Talk about a clear view!

36 The deep-sea anglerfish has a special hinge in its jaw that allows it to swallow prey twice its size. That's one big bite!

37 Sea otters have the densest fur of any animal, with up to 1 million hairs per square inch. It's like wearing the world's fluffiest coat!

38 The mimic octopus can change its shape, color, and behavior to imitate other sea creatures. It's like the master of underwater disguises!

39 The frilled shark has over 300 teeth arranged in 25 rows. It's like a living, swimming chainsaw!

40 The Christmas tree worm gets its name from its colorful, spiral-shaped gills that resemble the branches of a Christmas tree. It's like a festive, underwater decoration!

41 The leatherback sea turtle is the largest sea turtle, weighing up to 1,500 pounds. It's like a giant, swimming tank!

42 The fangtooth fish has the largest teeth of any fish its size. It's like having a mouth full of daggers!

43 The blanket octopus can unfurl its arms like a giant, underwater cape to scare off predators. It's like a superhero of the sea!

44 The marine iguana, found only in the Galápagos Islands, is the only lizard that can swim in the ocean. It's like a living, swimming Godzilla!

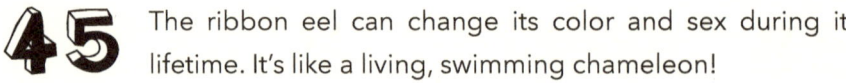

45 The ribbon eel can change its color and sex during its lifetime. It's like a living, swimming chameleon!

46 The vampire squid has large, red eyes and webbed arms that it can use to envelop its prey. It's like a spooky, underwater Dracula!

47 The sawfish has a long, flat snout lined with sharp teeth that it uses to slash through prey. It's like having a built-in saw for a nose!

48 The gulper eel has a massive mouth that can open wide enough to swallow prey larger than itself. It's like a living, swimming trash compactor!

49 Clownfish and sea anemones have a special relationship, where the clownfish protects the anemone from predators, and the anemone provides the clownfish with a safe home. It's like the ultimate underwater friendship!

50 The deep-sea hatchetfish gets its name from its thin, flat body that resembles the blade of a hatchet. It's like a swimming, underwater axe!

INVENTIONS AND DISCOVERIES

1 Did you know that the first chocolate bar was invented in 1847 by Joseph Fry? Thank goodness for chocolate!

2 The first ice cream cone was created at the 1904 World's Fair when a vendor ran out of bowls and teamed up with a waffle maker. Talk about a sweet collaboration!

3 The first potato chips were invented by George Crum in 1853 after a customer complained that his french fries were too thick. Sometimes, accidents lead to the tastiest inventions!

4 The first recorded use of toilet paper dates back to 6th century China. Before that, people had to get pretty creative!

5 The first traffic light was installed in London in 1868, but it exploded less than a month later. It took a while for traffic lights to catch on after that!

6 The first version of the internet, called ARPANET, was created in 1969. It was a far cry from the worldwide web we know today!

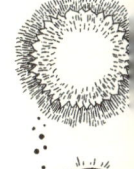

7 The first mobile phone call was made in 1973 by Martin Cooper. Can you imagine carrying around a phone the size of a brick?

8 Bubble wrap was originally invented as wallpaper, but it was much more fun to pop than to put on walls!

9 The first pair of eyeglasses was invented in Italy around 1286. People must have been squinting a lot before that!

10 The first vending machine was invented in Ancient Egypt around 215 BCE. It dispensed holy water in exchange for coins. Talk about an ancient convenience!

11 The first zippers were invented in 1893, but they weren't used in clothing until the 1930s. Before that, buttons ruled the fashion world!

12 The first microwave oven was invented in 1946 by Percy Spencer when he accidentally melted a candy bar in his pocket. It's like discovering a superpower!

13 The first mechanical alarm clock was invented in 1787 by Levi Hutchins. Before that, people had to rely on roosters or the sun to wake up!

14 The first bicycle was invented in 1817 by Karl von Drais. It had no pedals and was powered by the rider pushing it along with their feet. It's like a Flintstones car on two wheels!

15 The first skateboard was created in the 1950s by surfers who wanted to "surf" on land. It's like riding a wave without getting wet!

16 The first rubber eraser was invented in 1770 by Edward Nairne. Before that, people used bread crumbs or wax to erase their mistakes!

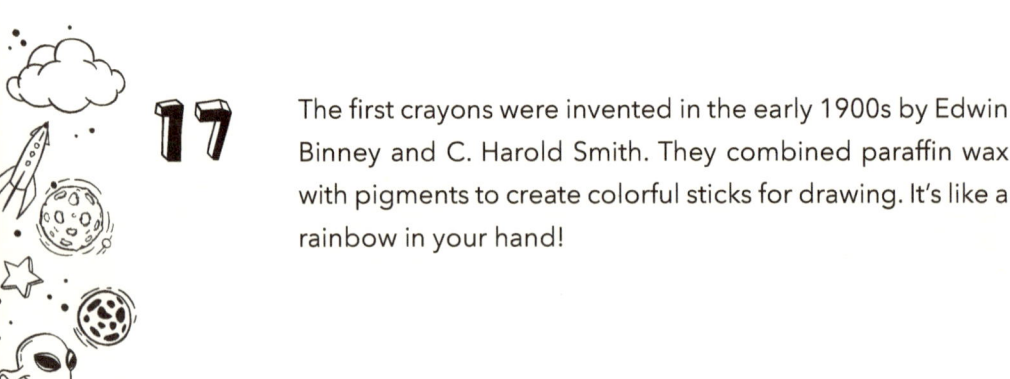

17 The first crayons were invented in the early 1900s by Edwin Binney and C. Harold Smith. They combined paraffin wax with pigments to create colorful sticks for drawing. It's like a rainbow in your hand!

18 The first video game, called "Tennis for Two," was invented in 1958 by William Higinbotham. It was played on an oscilloscope, a device used to display electrical signals. Talk about a blast from the past!

19 The first 3D movie was released in 1922, called "The Power of Love." The audience had to wear special glasses to see the 3D effects. It's like stepping into another dimension!

20 The first computer mouse was invented in 1964 by Douglas Engelbart. It was made of wood and had only one button. Can you imagine a mouse without a right-click?

21 The first airplane was invented by the Wright brothers in 1903. Their first flight lasted only 12 seconds and covered 120 feet. It's like a giant leap for mankind!

22 The first vacuum cleaner was invented in 1901 by Hubert Cecil Booth. It was so big that it had to be pulled by a horse and parked outside the house to be cleaned. Talk about heavy-duty cleaning!

23 The first electric toothbrush was invented in 1954 by Dr. Philippe Guy Woog. It's like having a tiny, spinning brush inside your mouth!

24 The first recipe for popcorn dates back to 16th century Aztec culture. People have been munching on this tasty treat for centuries!

25 The first roller coaster was built in 1884 at Coney Island in New York. It was called the Switchback Railway and reached a thrilling top speed of 6 miles per hour. Hold on tight!

26 The first ballpoint pen was invented in 1938 by László Bíró, a Hungarian journalist. No more messy ink spills!

27 The first digital camera was invented in 1975 by Steven Sasson, an engineer at Kodak. It weighed 8 pounds and took 23 seconds to capture a single image. Can you say "Cheese" that long?

28 The first cell phone, the Motorola DynaTAC, was released in 1983. It cost nearly $4,000 and had a battery life of just 30 minutes. That's one pricey phone call!

29 The first disposable diaper was invented in 1947 by Marion Donovan. It was called the "Boater" and was made of waterproof plastic. Talk about a game-changer for parents!

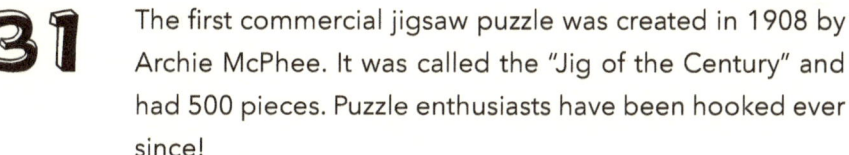

30 The first television was invented in the 1920s by John Logie Baird. Early televisions were mechanical and had a spinning disk with holes to create the image. It's like watching TV in slow motion!

31 The first commercial jigsaw puzzle was created in 1908 by Archie McPhee. It was called the "Jig of the Century" and had 500 pieces. Puzzle enthusiasts have been hooked ever since!

32 The first electric washing machine was invented in 1908 by Alva J. Fisher. It was called the "Thor" and looked like a large wooden barrel. Laundry day just got a whole lot easier!

33 The first mechanical clock was invented in China in the 8th century by a monk named Yi Xing. It was powered by water and used a series of gears to keep time. Tick-tock!

34 The first traffic cones were invented in 1940 by Charles D. Scanlon, an American painter. They were originally made of wood and used to keep cars away from wet paint. Talk about a bright idea!

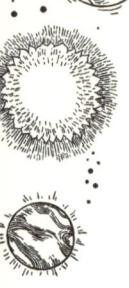

35 The first practical refrigerator was invented in 1913 by Fred W. Wolf. It was called the "Domelre," short for "Domestic Electric Refrigerator." No more iceboxes!

36 The first electric toaster was invented in 1893 by George Schneider and Albert Marsh. It was called the "Eclipse" and could toast only one side of the bread at a time. Can you imagine breakfast without toast!?

37 The first escalator was invented in 1891 by Jesse W. Reno. It was called the "inclined elevator" and was used as an amusement park ride. Talk about a fun way to go up!

38 The first typewriter was invented in 1868 by Christopher Latham Sholes. It was called the Sholes and Glidden Type-Writer, and the QWERTY keyboard layout we still use today was developed for it. Clickety-clack!

39 The first rubber band was invented in 1845 by Stephen Perry, a British inventor. They were originally made from vulcanized rubber, and now they're essential office supplies!

40 The first recorded recipe for s'mores dates back to 1927 in a Girl Scouts guidebook. Campfires and gooey marshmallow treats have been a perfect match ever since!

41 The first modern trampoline was invented in 1936 by George Nissen and Larry Griswold. It was initially used to train tumblers and astronauts. Bounce your way to the stars!

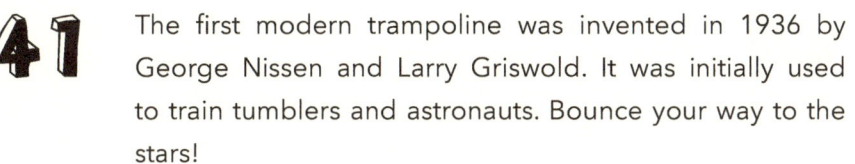

42 The first automatic dishwasher was invented in 1886 by Josephine Cochrane, a wealthy socialite who was tired of her dishes being chipped by her servants. Talk about a labor-saving device!

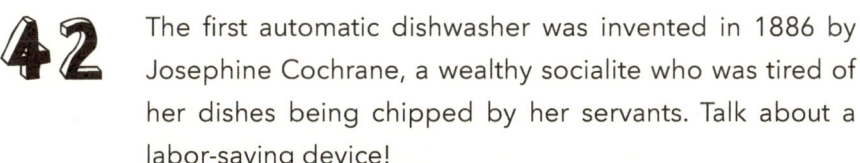

43 The first photocopier, called the Xerox 914, was invented in 1959 by Chester Carlson. It revolutionized the way we share and reproduce documents. Copy that!

44 The first solar-powered calculator was invented in 1978 by Sharp Corporation. It's like doing math with the power of the sun!

45 The first electric iron was invented in 1882 by Henry W. Seeley. It was called the "electric flatiron" and made ironing clothes a breeze!

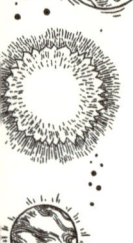

46 The first chewing gum was invented in 1848 by John B. Curtis. It was made from the sap of the spruce tree and called "State of Maine Pure Spruce Gum." Chew on that!

47 The first email was sent in 1971 by Ray Tomlinson, an American computer programmer. He used the "@" symbol to separate the user's name from the computer's name. And now, we can't imagine life without it!

48 The first electric blender was invented in 1922 by Stephen Poplawski. He wanted to make it easier to mix malted milk drinks, but little did he know he'd change the way we make smoothies and milkshakes forever!

49 The first metal detector was invented in 1881 by Alexander Graham Bell. He created it to find a bullet lodged in President James Garfield after an assassination attempt. Now they help us find buried treasure and lost keys!

50 The first modern hair dryer was invented in 1920 by Alexandre Godefroy, a French hairdresser. Before that, women had to use vacuum cleaners to dry their hair. Talk about a bad hair day!

FOOD AND BEVERAGE

1 Did you know that tomatoes were once considered poisonous? It's a good thing we figured out they're delicious and safe to eat!

2 The world's largest chocolate chip cookie was made in South Carolina and weighed 40,000 pounds. It had a diameter of 101 feet. Wowzers!

3 The world's largest mozzarella cheese stick was made in New York and measured 6,463 feet long. It was created using over 2,000 pounds of cheese. That's the weight of a small car!

4 The world's largest ice cream cake was made in Canada and weighed 21,000 pounds. That's as heavy as a garbage truck!

5 The largest pizza ever made was 131 feet from end to end and weighed over 51,000 pounds. That's a pizza party for the record books!

6 Fortune cookies were actually invented in California, not China! Talk about a surprising twist of fate!

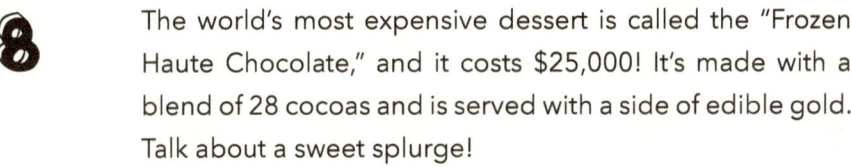

7 The popsicle was invented by an 11-year-old boy named Frank Epperson in 1905. He accidentally left a mixture of soda water and powdered flavoring outside overnight with a stirring stick in it, and it froze. Yum!

8 The world's most expensive dessert is called the "Frozen Haute Chocolate," and it costs $25,000! It's made with a blend of 28 cocoas and is served with a side of edible gold. Talk about a sweet splurge!

9 The sandwich was supposedly invented by the Earl of Sandwich, who wanted a convenient way to eat while playing cards. It's like a portable meal you can hold in one hand!

10 Cotton candy was invented by a dentist named William Morrison. Maybe he just wanted more business!

11 The game of chess is believed to have originated in India around the 6th century. It's a game of strategy and skill that has been played for centuries. Checkmate!

12 The world's largest omelette was made in Portugal and used over 145,000 eggs. That's a lot of scrambling!

13 Did you know that apples are part of the rose family? Talk about a rosy surprise!

14 The largest chocolate bar ever made weighed over 12,770 pounds. That's one giant chocolate craving satisfied!

15 The tallest ice cream cone ever made measured over 10 feet tall. You'd need a really long spoon to eat that!

16 The world's largest taco weighed 1,654 pounds and was made in Mexico. It's like a fiesta for your taste buds!

17 The world's largest sushi roll was made in Russia and was over 1.5 miles long. It's like a sushi train that never ends!

18 The world's largest hamburger weighed 2,014 pounds and was made in Minnesota. You'd need a giant bun to go with that patty!

19 The largest cup of coffee ever brewed contained over 18,000 gallons of coffee. That's enough to keep you awake for a lifetime!

20 The world's largest milkshake contained 6,000 gallons of ice cream and milk. It's like a swimming pool filled with deliciousness!

21 The world's longest noodle was 1.9 miles long. It's like a noodle marathon!

22 The world's largest teapot can hold over 1,102 gallons of tea. That's enough for a massive tea party!

23 The largest serving of scrambled eggs was made in Colombia and used over 62,000 eggs. Talk about an egg-cellent feast!

24 The world's largest bowl of soup was made in Honduras and contained over 2,500 gallons of soup. It's like a bathtub filled with delicious broth!

25 The world's largest cake weighed over 33,000 pounds and was made in Indonesia. Let them eat (giant) cake!

26 The world's largest pretzel was made in Germany and weighed over 1,700 pounds. It's like a salty, twisty mountain!

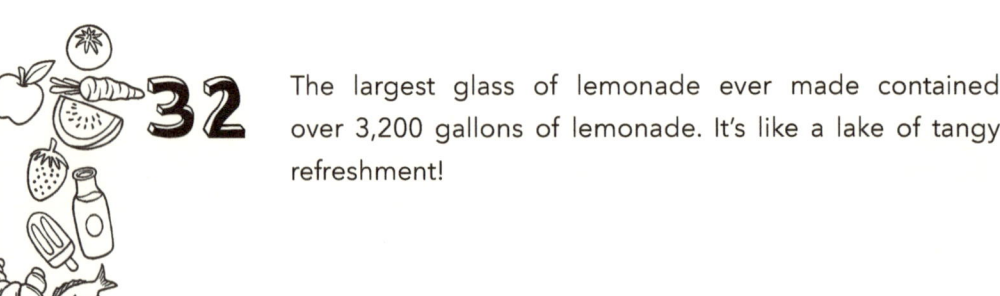

27 The largest bowl of pasta was made in Italy and contained over 17,000 pounds of noodles and sauce. That's a pasta lover's dream come true!

28 The world's largest cupcake weighed over 2,000 pounds and was made in Michigan. It's like a sweet, gigantic treat!

29 The largest loaf of bread ever made weighed a whopping 3,463 pounds and was baked in Italy. It's like a bread pillow you can sleep on!

30 The world's largest cheesecake was made in Mexico and weighed over 4,700 pounds. It's a creamy, dreamy delight!

31 The world's largest plate of nachos weighed 5,039 pounds and was made in Kansas. Pass the cheese, please!

32 The largest glass of lemonade ever made contained over 3,200 gallons of lemonade. It's like a lake of tangy refreshment!

33 The largest bowl of salad ever made weighed over 44,000 pounds and was created in Romania. Talk about a healthy feast!

34 The world's largest smoothie was made in New Zealand and contained over 5,800 gallons of blended fruit goodness. It's a fruit explosion!

35 Did you know that popcorn has been enjoyed as a snack for over 5,000 years? It's an ancient treat that never goes out of style!

36 The largest cup of hot chocolate ever made contained 880 gallons of hot cocoa. It's like a cozy, warm hug in a cup!

37 The world's largest serving of mashed potatoes weighed over 3,000 pounds and was made in Belgium. That's a mountain of creamy, buttery goodness!

38 The world's largest meatball was made in South Dakota and weighed over 1,100 pounds. It's like a giant, meaty snowball!

39 The largest pitcher of iced tea ever made contained 1,720 gallons of refreshing tea. It's like a waterfall of cool, tasty beverages!

40 The world's largest ice cream sandwich weighed over 2,400 pounds and was made in California. It's like a chilly, sweet skyscraper!

41 The largest scoop of ice cream ever made weighed over 3,000 pounds and was created in New York. It's a massive, frosty treat!

42 The world's largest bowl of chili was made in Texas and contained over 2,100 gallons of spicy deliciousness. It's like a volcano of flavor!

43 The largest glass of wine ever poured contained over 1,100 gallons of wine. Cheers to a giant celebration!

44 The world's largest potato chip was 25 inches long and was made in the United Kingdom. It's a crispy, salty sensation!

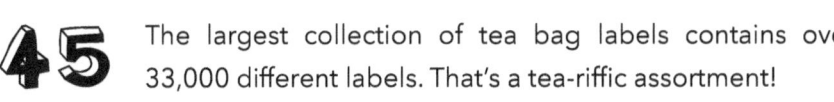

45 The largest collection of tea bag labels contains over 33,000 different labels. That's a tea-riffic assortment!

46 The world's largest doughnut was made in New York and weighed over 1,700 pounds. It's like a sweet, doughy hula hoop!

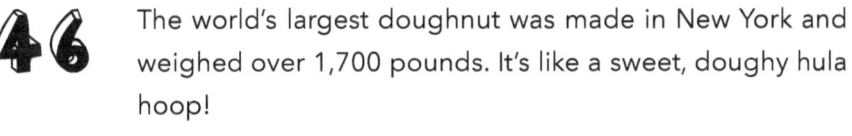

47 The largest piece of toffee ever made weighed over 5,000 pounds and was created in Norway. It's a sticky, sugary sensation!

48 The world's largest gingerbread house was made in Texas and measured over 2,500 square feet. It's a spicy, sweet mansion!

49 The largest serving of fish and chips ever made weighed over 1,000 pounds and was created in England. It's like a feast from the sea!

50 The largest bowl of cereal ever made contained over 2,600 gallons of milk and cereal, and it was created in the United States in 2008. That's enough cereal to feed a small town!

SPORTS AND GAMES

1 The state of Florida is so flat that if you stood on a pancake, it would be hillier than Florida! Now that's a tasty comparison!

2 The most push-ups completed in one hour is 2,919, achieved by Jarrad Young in 2020. That's a whole lot of muscle power!

3 The most cartwheels completed in one hour is 1,101, achieved by Ashrita Furman in 2011. Flipping fantastic!

4 The world's oldest known board game is called Senet, which originated in ancient Egypt around 3100 BCE. It's like a blast from the past!

5 The world's largest game of dodgeball involved 6,084 participants in 2012. That's one epic dodgeball battle!

6 The shortest professional boxer in history was Jacob "Baby Jake" Matlala, who stood at just 4 feet 10 inches tall. Don't underestimate his punch!

7 The game of soccer, also known as football, is played by an estimated 270 million people worldwide. That's a whole lot

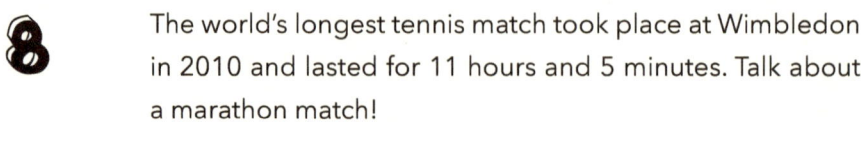

of goal scoring!

8 The world's longest tennis match took place at Wimbledon in 2010 and lasted for 11 hours and 5 minutes. Talk about a marathon match!

9 The highest score ever achieved in a single game of bowling is 300 points, known as a perfect game. That's 12 consecutive strikes in a row!

10 The fastest recorded serve in tennis was hit by Samuel Groth at a speed of 163.7 miles per hour. You'd need lightning-fast reflexes to return that ball!

11 The game of chess is believed to have originated in India around the 6th century. It's a game of strategy and skill that has been played for centuries.

12 The world's largest game of musical chairs involved 8,238 participants in 1989. Talk about a big game of musical madness!

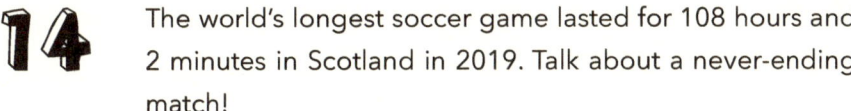

13 The world's highest tightrope walk took place at an altitude of 17,716 feet above sea level in the French Alps. That's like walking on a thin wire in the sky!

14 The world's longest soccer game lasted for 108 hours and 2 minutes in Scotland in 2019. Talk about a never-ending match!

15 The world's largest game of capture the flag involved 2,888 participants in 2016. It's like a giant game of stealth and strategy!

16 The world's largest hopscotch game covered an area of 89,000 square feet and was created in Canada in 2016. Hop, skip, and jump your way to fun!

17 The world's largest game of Twister featured 4,160 players and was played on a mat that covered 100,000 square feet. It's like a giant, colorful puzzle of human bodies!

18 The world's largest game of tag involved 2,202 participants in 2013. You're it!

19 The highest score ever recorded in a game of Scrabble is 830 points. Talk about a word wizard!

20 The world's largest game of Simon Says involved 12,215 participants in 2007. Better listen closely and follow those instructions!

21 The fastest recorded sprint speed was achieved by Usain Bolt, who reached a speed of 27.8 miles per hour. It's like having a lightning bolt on the field!

22 The most goals scored in a single ice hockey game by one player is 7, accomplished by Joe Malone in 1920. That's a scoring spree!

23 The world's largest game of leapfrog involved 1,300 participants in 2011. That's a whole lot of jumping and ducking!

24 The world's largest human pyramid was created in Spain in 2016 and involved 1,202 participants. Talk about teamwork and balance!

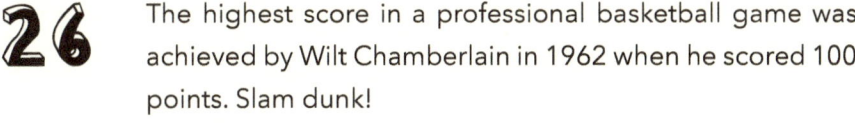

25 The fastest 100-meter hurdles wearing swim fins was completed in 14.82 seconds by Veronica Torr in 2009. That's one speedy, flippered sprint!

26 The highest score in a professional basketball game was achieved by Wilt Chamberlain in 1962 when he scored 100 points. Slam dunk!

27 The longest golf drive ever recorded was made by Mike Austin in 1974, and the ball traveled 515 yards. That's more than a quarter of a mile!

28 The most goals scored in a game of water polo by a single player is 13, achieved by Carlos Correa in 1980. Splash and score!

29 The world's largest game of Duck, Duck, Goose involved 2,135 participants in 2011. Duck, duck, run!

30 The longest domino chain reaction consisted of 277,275 dominoes and took 15 people 2 months to set up. That's like a never-ending line of falling fun!

31 The world's largest game of hide-and-seek involved 1,437 participants in 2010. Ready or not, here they come!

32 The longest game of Monopoly ever played lasted for 70 consecutive days. It's like a never-ending battle of property and wealth!

33 The world's largest hopper ball race involved 294 participants in 2012. Bounce your way to the finish line!

34 The longest marathon playing baseball lasted for 82 hours and 5 minutes and involved 105 players in 2015. Batter up for a long game!

35 The world's largest game of Red Rover involved 1,119 participants in 2008. Red Rover, Red Rover, send everyone right over!

36 The most home runs hit in a single Major League Baseball season is 73, achieved by Barry Bonds in 2001. Home run king!

37 The longest game of underwater hockey lasted for 50 hours and 10 minutes and involved 58 players in 2016. It's like playing hockey in an underwater world!

38 The world's largest game of freeze tag involved 634 participants in 2008. Freeze and unfreeze in a giant game of fun!

39 The most juggling catches made while blindfolded in one minute is 94, achieved by Anthony Gatto in 2010. Talk about juggling in the dark!

40 The world's largest game of musical statues involved 1,116 participants in 2011. Dance and freeze to the beat!

41 The longest recorded discus throw was made by Jürgen Schult in 1986, and the discus traveled 243 feet. That's a far-flying disc!

42 The world's largest game of rock-paper-scissors involved 2,950 participants in 2012. It's like a massive game of hand gesture battles!

43 The most consecutive wins in professional boxing is 89, achieved by Julio Cesar Chavez from 1980 to 1993. That's a knockout streak!

44 The longest game of kickball lasted for 69 hours and involved 36 players in 2015. It's like a never-ending game of kick and run!

45 The world's largest game of Follow the Leader involved 952 participants in 2010. Follow along in a giant game of copycat!

46 The fastest time to complete a marathon while dribbling a basketball is 4 hours, 10 minutes, and 44 seconds, achieved by Darren Weissman in 2013. It's like running a marathon and playing basketball at the same time!

47 The world's largest human foosball game involved 862 participants in 2015. It's like playing foosball with real people as the players!

48 The world's largest game of beach ball volleyball involved 1,693 participants in 2010. It's like a giant game of bouncy, beach fun!

49 The longest game of touch football lasted for 52 hours and involved 36 players in 2014. It's like a never-ending game of pass and run!

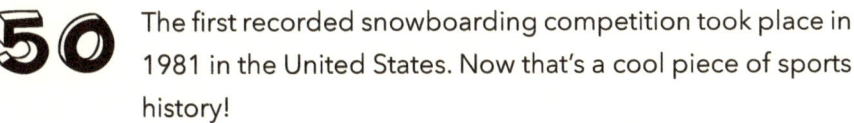

50 The first recorded snowboarding competition took place in 1981 in the United States. Now that's a cool piece of sports history!

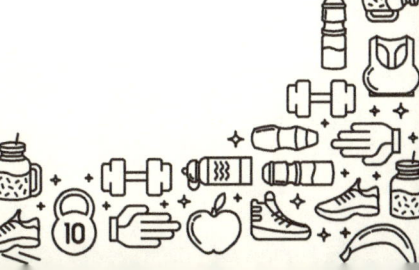

WORLD RECORDS

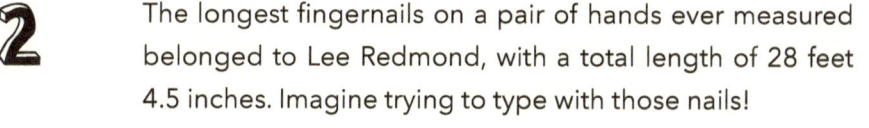

1 The world's largest rubber band ball was created by Joel Waul in the United States and weighs 9,032 pounds. It's like a giant, bouncy rubber planet!

2 The longest fingernails on a pair of hands ever measured belonged to Lee Redmond, with a total length of 28 feet 4.5 inches. Imagine trying to type with those nails!

3 The world's largest collection of rubber ducks is owned by Charlotte Lee and consists of over 9,000 different ducks. It's a quacky assortment!

4 The world's tallest sandcastle was built in Germany in 2019 and measured 57 feet 11 inches tall. It's a sandy skyscraper!

5 The world's largest gathering of people dressed as Smurfs consisted of 2,762 participants in Wales in 2009. It's like a village of blue, friendly folks!

6 The world's largest human mattress dominoes involved 2,019 participants and took place in the United States in 2016. It's a cozy, tumbling chain reaction!

7 The largest collection of traffic cones belongs to David Morgan, who owns 137 different traffic cones. It's a conical wonderland!

8 The most Big Macs eaten by one person is over 32,000, consumed by Donald A. Gorske since 1972. That's a lifetime of fast-food feasting!

9 The world's largest knitting needles are 14 feet long and were used to knit a tension square. Talk about supersized knitting!

10 The world's largest snowball fight involved 7,681 participants and took place in Canada in 2016. It's a frosty, flurry-filled battle!

11 The most tattoos received in 24 hours by a single person is 801, achieved by Hollis Cantrell in 2008. That's a whole lot of ink!

12 The world's longest scarf was knitted by Helge Johansen and measures 3,463 miles long. It's like a never-ending, cozy embrace!

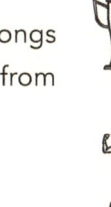

13 The world's largest collection of toothpaste tubes belongs to Dr. Val Kolpakov and consists of over 2,000 tubes from around the world. It's a minty, fresh assortment!

14 The largest gathering of people dressed as penguins was 972 participants in the United Kingdom in 2015. It's like a waddling, black and white party!

15 The world's longest paperclip chain was created by Fettes College students and measures 55,507 feet long. That's a whole lot of linked-up paperclips!

16 The most people hula-hooping simultaneously was 4,183 participants in Thailand in 2013. It's a hip-swinging, hoop-spinning extravaganza!

17 The world's largest collection of rubber bands is owned by Suresh Joachim and consists of over 1 million bands. It's a stretchy, colorful collection!

18 The world's longest beard belonged to Hans Langseth and measured 17 feet 6 inches long. Talk about an impressive facial hair feat!

19 The largest collection of Barbie dolls belongs to Bettina Dorfmann, with over 15,000 unique dolls. It's a fashionable, plastic paradise!

20 The world's largest gathering of people dressed as Superman was 867 participants in the United Kingdom in 2013. It's like a heroic, flying spectacle!

21 The most people simultaneously blowing bubbles with chewing gum was 738 participants in Argentina in 2007. It's a bubbly, sticky explosion!

22 The largest collection of rubber chickens belongs to Dee Dee Dunleavy and consists of over 900 squawking, rubbery fowls. It's a hilariously noisy assortment!

23 The world's largest whoopee cushion measured 25 feet 5 inches in diameter and was created in the United States in 2017. That's one giant, hilarious surprise!

24 The most people dancing with hula hoops was 4,880 participants in Japan in 2018. It's a hip-shaking, hula-hooping dance party!

25 The most people crammed into a single car was 31 participants in Australia in 2012. Talk about a cozy car ride!

26 The world's largest rubber duck measured 61 feet tall and floated on a lake in Canada in 2017. It's a massive, adorable, yellow companion!

27 The world's largest gathering of people dressed as zombies was 15,458 participants in the United States in 2012. It's a spooky, undead mob!

28 The most people wearing Groucho Marx glasses simultaneously was 4,436 participants in the United States in 2009. It's a funny-faced, bespectacled crowd!

29 The world's largest collection of troll dolls belongs to Sherry Groom and consists of over 8,000 grinning, hairy figurines. It's a tiny, troll-filled wonderland!

30 The most people simultaneously throwing pies was 4,961 participants in the United States in 2016. It's a messy, delicious food fight!

31 The most people skipping rope simultaneously was 1,881 participants in Australia in 2012. It's a high-flying, jump-roping extravaganza!

32 The world's longest mustache belonged to Ram Singh Chauhan and measured 14 feet long. That's one impressive, hairy accomplishment!

33 The world's largest gathering of people dressed as gorillas was 1,061 participants in the United Kingdom in 2013. It's like a wild, furry jungle party!

34 The most people wearing fake mustaches simultaneously was 6,471 participants in the United States in 2013. It's a disguise-filled, mustachioed mob!

35 The most people dressed as fruits and vegetables was 888 participants in the United States in 2012. It's a colorful, nutritious costume party!

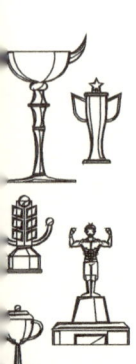

36 The largest collection of rubber stamps belongs to Petra Engels and consists of over 4,000 unique stamps. It's a stamp-filled, ink-splattered assortment!

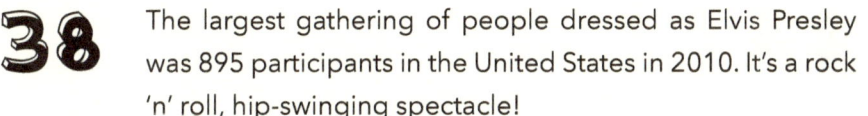

37 The most people wearing balloon hats simultaneously was 6,129 participants in the United States in 2011. It's an inflated, colorful headwear extravaganza!

38 The largest gathering of people dressed as Elvis Presley was 895 participants in the United States in 2010. It's a rock 'n' roll, hip-swinging spectacle!

39 The world's largest collection of rubber snakes belongs to Clint Pustejovsky and consists of over 3,000 slithering, rubber reptiles. It's a wriggling, hissing assortment!

40 The most people wearing sunglasses in the dark simultaneously was 27,000 participants in the United States in 2015. It's a shady, mysterious mob!

41 The most people making sand angels simultaneously was 1,387 participants in the United States in 2017. It's like creating a sandy, heavenly host on the beach!

42 The most people wearing false teeth simultaneously was 1,950 participants in the United States in 2010. It's a chattering, toothy crowd!

43 The world's largest collection of miniature chairs belongs to Barbara Hartsfield and consists of over 3,000 tiny seats. It's a small, sit-able wonderland!

44 The most people dressed as mummies was 2,529 participants in the United States in 2010. It's like a bandage-wrapped, ancient Egyptian gathering!

45 The largest gathering of people dressed as pirates was 14,231 participants in the United Kingdom in 2012. It's a swashbuckling, sea-faring party!

46 The most people wearing sock puppets simultaneously was 2,605 participants in the United States in 2011. It's a fuzzy, expressive puppet extravaganza!

47 The most people wearing paper crowns simultaneously was 6,084 participants in the United States in 2012. It's a regal, paper-crowned gathering!

48 The largest gathering of people dressed as witches was 1,607 participants in Spain in 2010. It's a magical, spell-casting assembly!

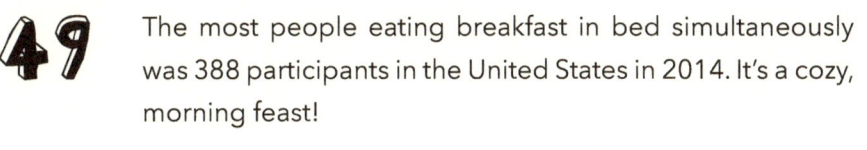

49 The most people eating breakfast in bed simultaneously was 388 participants in the United States in 2014. It's a cozy, morning feast!

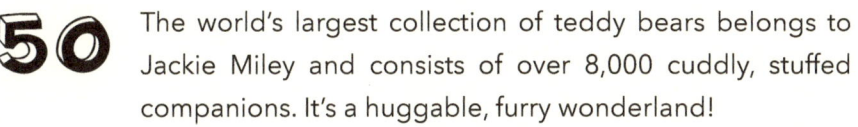

50 The world's largest collection of teddy bears belongs to Jackie Miley and consists of over 8,000 cuddly, stuffed companions. It's a huggable, furry wonderland!

GEOGRAPHY AND LANDMARKS

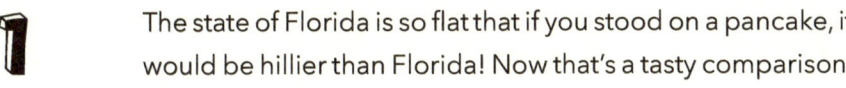

1 The state of Florida is so flat that if you stood on a pancake, it would be hillier than Florida! Now that's a tasty comparison.

2 There's a town in Norway called "Hell," and it actually freezes over every winter! So, when someone says, "When Hell freezes over," it really does!

3 In Japan, there's a festival called Kanamara Matsuri, where people celebrate with unusual pink wooden sculptures. It's a one-of-a-kind party!

4 There's a place in Canada called "Saint-Louis-du-Ha! Ha!" and it's the only town with two exclamation points in its name. That's double the excitement!

5 The city of Istanbul, Turkey, is the only city in the world that spans two continents: Europe and Asia. It's like being in two places at once – talk about a split personality!

6 There's an island in the Bahamas called "Pig Beach" where wild pigs swim and play with tourists. No need to hog the beach, though; there's plenty of space for everyone!

7 The world's tallest mountain, Mount Everest, has a lot of snow and ice. Climbers often leave behind a snowman to mark their adventure – just watch out for Frosty's chilly high-fives!

8 There's a town in Australia called "Nowhere Else." It's the only place you can say you're "Nowhere Else" and actually mean it!

9 The Great Wall of China is so long that if you turned it into a giant noodle, you could slurp it for years! Just don't forget the soy sauce.

10 The Leaning Tower of Pisa is famous for its tilt. It's like the world's biggest game of Jenga, but please, no one pull out a block!

11 The Amazon Rainforest is so dense that when it rains, it can take 10 minutes for the water to reach the ground. Talk about a slow-motion raindrop race!

12 The Grand Canyon is so big that if all the world's donkeys stood at the bottom, they still wouldn't be able to see out. Eeyore would be so disappointed.

13 Africa's Lake Victoria is so large, it could hold enough water to fill everyone's bathtub on Earth – that's a lot of rubber duckies!

14 There are more than 7,000 islands in the Caribbean Sea. If you visited one island per day, it would take you over 19 years to see them all! Better start packing.

15 The world's smallest country, Vatican City, is so tiny that you could fit it inside Central Park in New York City. It's a heavenly little hideaway!

16 The Great Blue Hole in Belize is so deep that it could hold the Eiffel Tower – and you'd still have room for a giant snorkel on top!

17 The world's largest salt flat, Salar de Uyuni in Bolivia, is so flat that if you put a giant pizza on it, there wouldn't be a single pepperoni out of place.

18 The Colosseum in Rome could hold 50,000 spectators. That's enough people to have a massive, ancient-world toga party!

19 The Great Barrier Reef in Australia is so big, it can be seen from space. Even astronauts need a good snorkeling spot!

20 The Sahara Desert is so hot that if you tried to fry an egg on the sand, it would probably sizzle faster than you could say "sunny-side up!"

21 The world's longest place name is a hill in New Zealand called "Taumatawhakatangihangakoauauotamatea-turipukakapikimaungahoronukupokaiwhenuakitanatahu." Try saying that three times fast!

22 The city of Venice, Italy, has no roads, only canals – so you'll never have to worry about getting stuck in traffic. Just watch out for boat jams!

23 The Eiffel Tower in Paris, France, was once considered an eyesore by locals. Today, it's the city's most famous landmark – proving that beauty really is in the eye of the baguette-holder!

24 There's a town in Wales, United Kingdom, with a name so long, it has 58 letters: Llanfairpwllgwyngyllgogerychwyrn-drobwllllantysiliogogogoch. Good luck fitting that on a postcard!

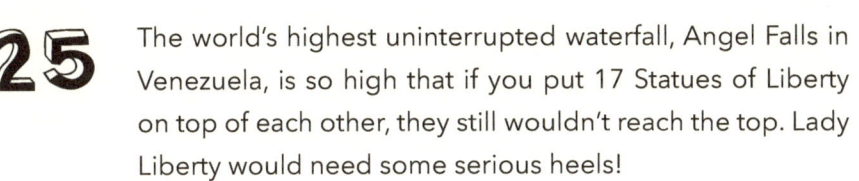

25 The world's highest uninterrupted waterfall, Angel Falls in Venezuela, is so high that if you put 17 Statues of Liberty on top of each other, they still wouldn't reach the top. Lady Liberty would need some serious heels!

26 The Galápagos Islands are home to a species of tortoise that can live for over 150 years. Talk about taking it slow and steady!

27 There's a village in the Netherlands called Giethoorn, where houses are only accessible by boat or on foot. It's like living in a real-life fairy tale – minus the singing mice.

28 The lowest point on Earth, the Dead Sea, is so salty that you can easily float on its surface. Just don't try tasting it – yuck!

29 The world's largest cave, Son Doong Cave in Vietnam, is so big that it could fit a 40-story skyscraper inside. Just imagine the size of the cave's bat signal!

30 The world's oldest tree, a bristlecone pine named Methuselah, is over 4,800 years old. It's been around longer than written history – talk about having some stories to tell!

31 The Bermuda Triangle is famous for mysterious disappearances of ships and planes. Some believe it's the work of aliens, but we think it might just be really bad GPS signals.

32 The world's largest tropical rainforest, the Amazon Rainforest, is home to a tribe that has never had contact with the outside world. We wonder if they've ever heard of fidget spinners!

33 The Great Sphinx of Giza in Egypt has the body of a lion and the head of a human. It's like the world's first attempt at a Halloween costume!

34 The world's smallest park, Mill Ends Park in Portland, Oregon, is only two feet wide – perfect for a romantic picnic for ants!

35 The world's largest beaver dam, located in Canada, is so big it can be seen from space. Those beavers must have been really busy!

36 The Grand Prismatic Spring in Yellowstone National Park, USA, has rainbow-colored waters caused by heat-loving bacteria. It's like a giant, steaming bowl of rainbow soup!

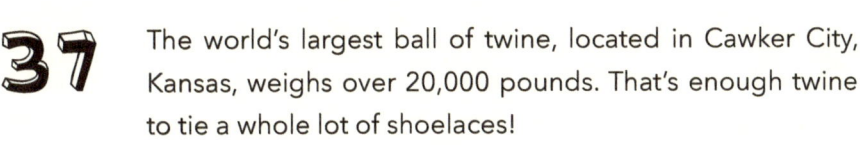

37 The world's largest ball of twine, located in Cawker City, Kansas, weighs over 20,000 pounds. That's enough twine to tie a whole lot of shoelaces!

38 There's a place in the Philippines called "Chocolate Hills," where over 1,200 grassy hills turn brown during the dry season. Sadly, they're not made of real chocolate.

39 The city of Siena, Italy, has a horse race called "Palio di Siena," where horses run around the city square. It's like a high-speed sightseeing tour on horseback!

40 The world's largest shoe, made of leather and wood, can be found in Marikina, Philippines. Cinderella would have a tough time losing that slipper!

41 The world's steepest street, Baldwin Street in New Zealand, has a 35% incline. Better hold onto your ice cream cone tightly or it might slide right out!

42 There's a place in California called "Glass Beach," where the sand is made up of tiny, smooth pieces of glass. It's a great place for a beach day – just don't forget your flip-flops!

43 In the Maldives, there's a beach called "Sea of Stars," where bioluminescent plankton create a magical, glowing effect in the water at night. It's like swimming in a galaxy far, far away!

44 The world's largest thermometer is located in Baker, California, and stands 134 feet tall. It's the perfect place to check if it's hot enough for a popsicle!

45 There's a city in India called "Shani Shingnapur" where houses have no doors. Knock, knock! Who's there? Nobody, apparently!

46 The Door to Hell in Turkmenistan has been on fire since 1971. That's like holding the world's longest marshmallow roast, but please don't get too close!

47 The world's largest pineapple-shaped building is located in South Africa. Now that's a fruity piece of architecture!

48 The world's largest ice cave, Eisriesenwelt in Austria, is so big that if you filled it with ice cream, you'd need a spoon the size of a bulldozer to dig in! Just don't forget the sprinkles.

49 In Portugal, there's a chapel called Capela dos Ossos, where the walls are decorated with bones and skulls. It's like a spooky pirate treasure map come to life!

50 The world's smallest volcano, the Taal Volcano in the Philippines, is so tiny that if it were a cake, it would be a cupcake. But beware, this tiny volcano has a fiery temper!

HUMAN BODY AND HEALTH

1 The human body contains enough blood vessels to wrap around the Earth more than twice! That's a long trip without a spaceship!

2 You grow about 590 miles of hair over your lifetime – that's like having a hairy road trip from New York City to Chicago!

3 Humans share 50% of their DNA with bananas. So, next time you slip on a banana peel, remember: it's practically family!

4 You blink around 28,800 times a day. That's like a never-ending game of peekaboo with the world!

5 The human body is made up of around 37 trillion cells. If they were dollar bills, you'd be a trillionaire 37 times over!

6 Sneezes can travel up to 100 miles per hour – faster than a cheetah on roller skates!

7 The human nose can remember 50,000 different scents. That's a lot of sniffing at the perfume counter!

8 Your heart beats around 100,000 times a day. It's like a never-ending drum solo in your chest!

9 You're taller in the morning than at night because the discs in your spine compress throughout the day. Talk about getting a good night's stretch!

10 Humans produce enough saliva in a lifetime to fill two swimming pools. Just don't dive in – eww!

11 Your brain can generate enough electricity to power a lightbulb. That's one bright idea!

12 The human body can produce 25 million new cells every second. It's like a cellular assembly line!

13 You shed about 40 pounds of skin in your lifetime – that's like shedding a whole kindergarten-sized kid!

14 The human body has over 600 muscles. Some of them are so tiny; they could win a muscle-minimizing contest!

15   Laughter really is the best medicine - it can boost your immune system, lower stress, and even help your heart. So, giggle your way to good health!

16   The world's loudest sneeze was 176 decibels. That's louder than a rock concert - achoo, rock on!

17   Your ears never stop growing throughout your life. You might end up looking like an elephant when you're older - minus the trunk!

18   The average person walks about 100,000 miles in a lifetime. That's like walking around the Earth four times - no passport required!

19   The average person will eat about 35 tons of food in their lifetime. That's like eating six elephants - talk about having a big appetite!

20   Your tongue print is as unique as your fingerprint. So, no licking crime scenes, please!

21 Your body is home to more bacteria than there are people on Earth. It's like you're the mayor of your very own microscopic city!

22 Your brain keeps developing until your late 40s. So, you can still teach an old brain new tricks!

23 The human eye can distinguish between 10 million different colors. That's a lot of shades of crayons!

24 The strongest muscle in your body is your jaw muscle. Just imagine how many jawbreakers you could chew through!

25 The longest hiccup attack ever recorded lasted for 68 years. That's one hiccup worth an entire lifetime!

26 The average person will spend about six months of their life brushing their teeth. Keep those pearly whites sparkling!

27 When you blush, the lining of your stomach blushes too. It's like a full-body embarrassment party!

28 Your bones are stronger than steel. You're basically a walking, talking superhero - just without the cape and spandex!

29 Your body has enough iron in it to make a 3-inch nail. You're practically a walking hardware store!

30 The human heart is about the size of your fist. Pump it up, heart-power!

31 You breathe in about 45 pounds of dust over your lifetime. It's like having a dusty party in your lungs!

32 Your feet contain a quarter of your body's bones. No wonder they get so tired after a long day of walking!

33 Your liver can regrow itself in just a few months. It's like having a superhero sidekick living inside you!

34 When you're awake, your brain generates enough heat to cook an egg. Talk about having egg on your brain!

35 The longest human hair ever recorded was over 18 feet long. That's like having a hair-rope to swing on!

36 The world's longest fingernails belonged to a woman named Lee Redmond, and they measured over 28 feet in total. That's a lot of nail polish!

37 The human body has 206 bones, but babies are born with around 270 bones. They fuse together as they grow – it's like a bony puzzle!

38 Humans are the only animals that cry tears when they're sad. So, go ahead and let it all out – you're only human!

39 The human body can survive without food for around three weeks, but only three days without water. Drink up, thirsty friends!

40 The average human will yawn around 250,000 times in their lifetime. That's a quarter-million yawn-versations!

41 Your fingernails grow faster on your dominant hand. It's like your body's way of giving you a high-five!

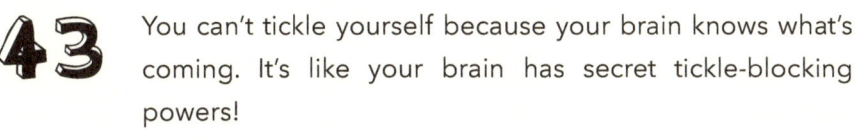

42 Your body is constantly replacing old cells with new ones. You're like a walking, talking science experiment!

43 You can't tickle yourself because your brain knows what's coming. It's like your brain has secret tickle-blocking powers!

44 Humans have a built-in GPS in their brains called the "hippocampus." It helps you remember where you've been and how to get there – most of the time!

45 The human body is about 60% water. So, technically, you're more than half mermaid or merman!

46 The world's loudest snorer was recorded at 92 decibels. That's like sleeping next to a running lawnmower!

47 The human body can detect taste in .0015 seconds – that's faster than the blink of an eye. Talk about fast food!

48 Your body gives off enough heat in 30 minutes to boil half a gallon of water. You're like a walking, talking teapot!

49 Your heart beats around 100,000 times a day, working tirelessly to keep you going. It's like your very own superhero, hidden inside your chest!

50 Your fingernails grow faster on your dominant hand. So, if you're right-handed, your right hand's nails are always trying to catch up with the left!

Dear reader,

First and foremost, I want to express my heartfelt gratitude for choosing my book to share with your little ones. I sincerely hope that you and your children have found joy, learning, and inspiration within these pages.

As an author, I pour my heart and soul into creating stories that not only entertain but also provide valuable lessons and experiences for your children. Your feedback is incredibly important to me and helps me to continue improving and creating content that resonates with young readers.

If you and your children have enjoyed reading this book and feel that it has added value to their lives, I kindly ask you to consider leaving a review.

I want you to know that I will personally read each and every review. Your thoughts and experiences mean a great deal to me. To make this process as seamless as possible, I have included a QR code here that you can scan, which will directly take you to the Amazon review page.

Thank you for your support and for giving my book a chance to spark imagination, wonder, and learning in your children's lives. I deeply appreciate it and look forward to continuing this journey together.

Warmest regards,

Riley Wolfe

Made in United States
Troutdale, OR
08/05/2023

11840205R00061